AF257039

Carnet de coloriage pour camions a ordures

Coloring Pages for Kids

Coloring Pages for Kids
An imprint of Ciparum LLC

Carnet de coloriage pour camions a ordures
© 2017 Ciparum LLC
All rights reserved.
ISBN-10:1-63589-501-4
ISBN-13:978-1-63589-501-8

Coloring Pages for Kids

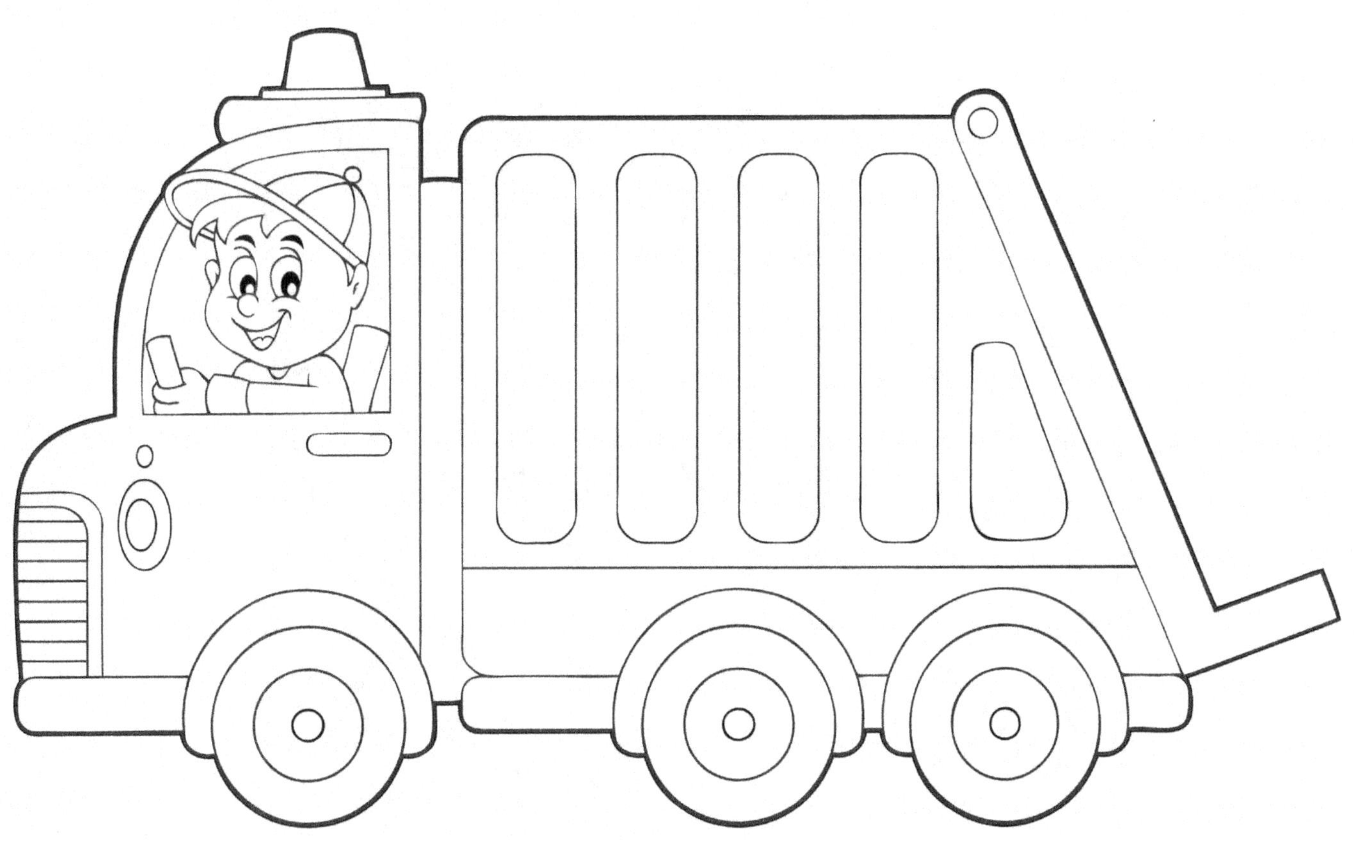

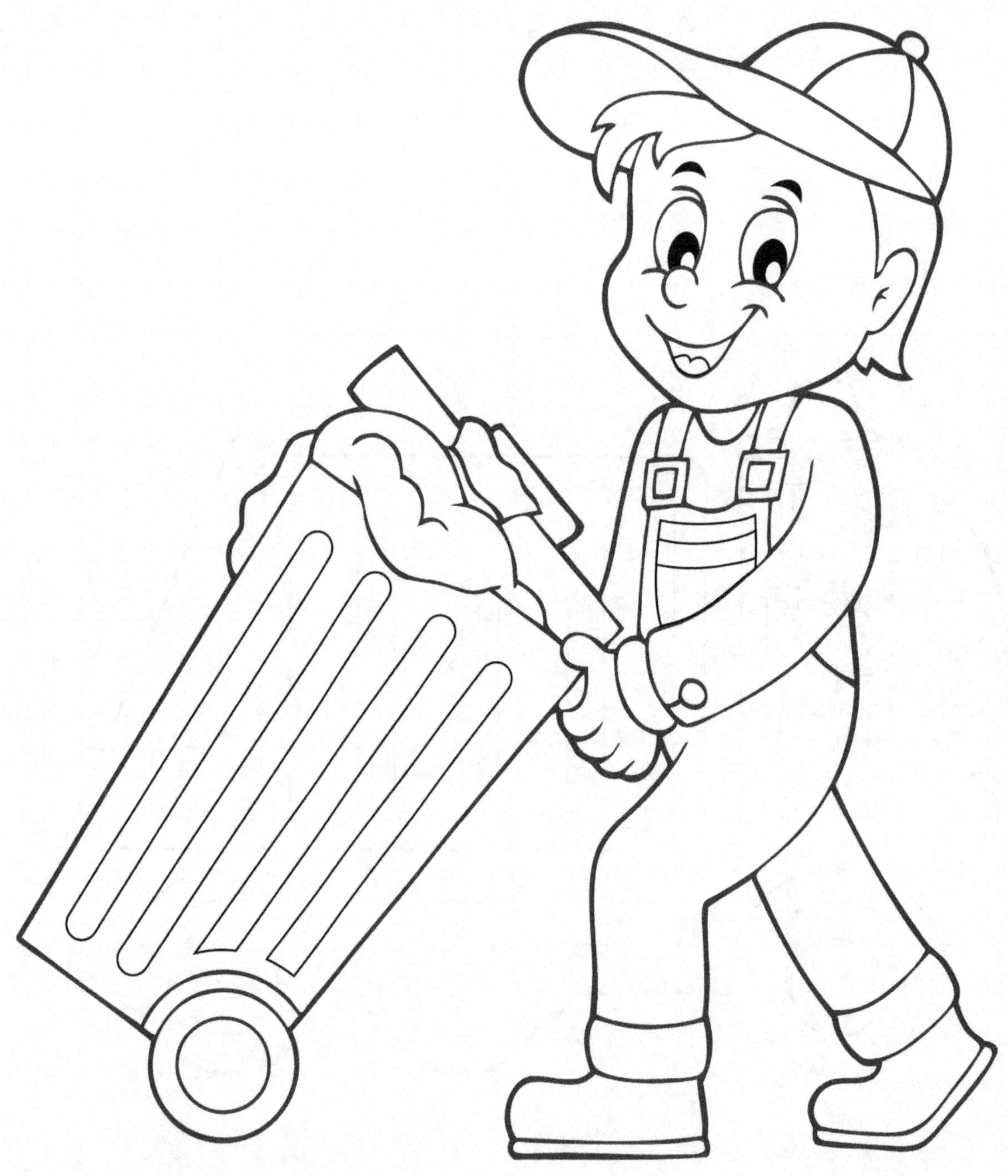

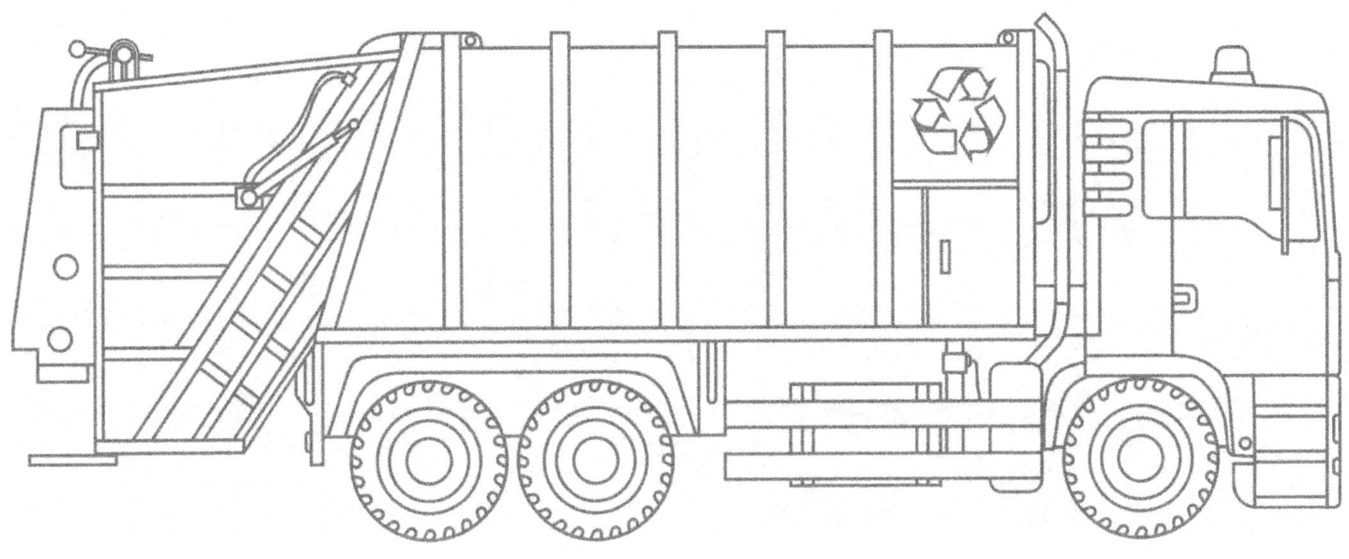

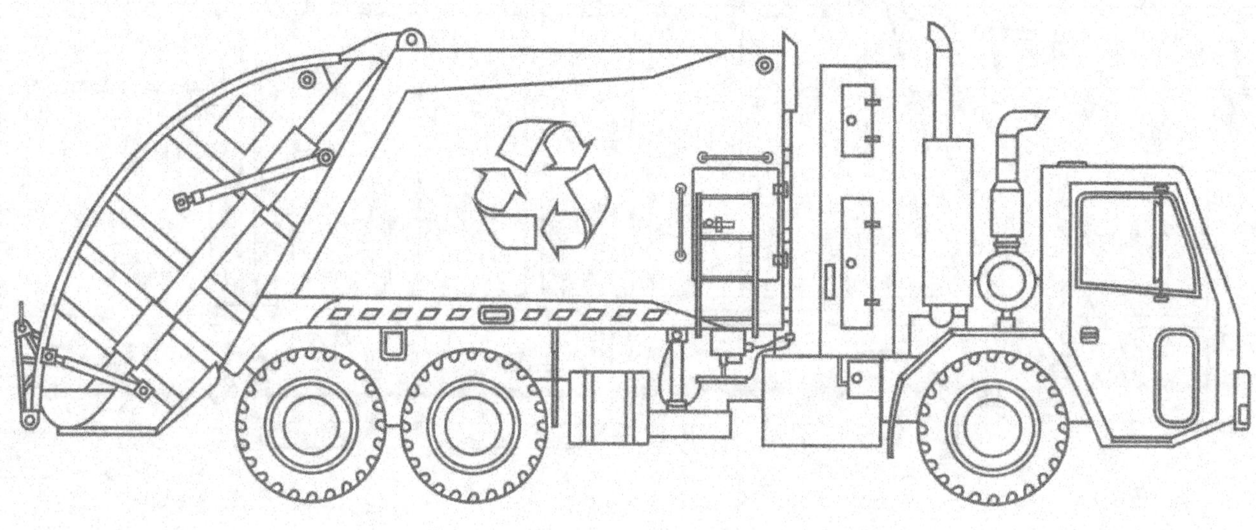

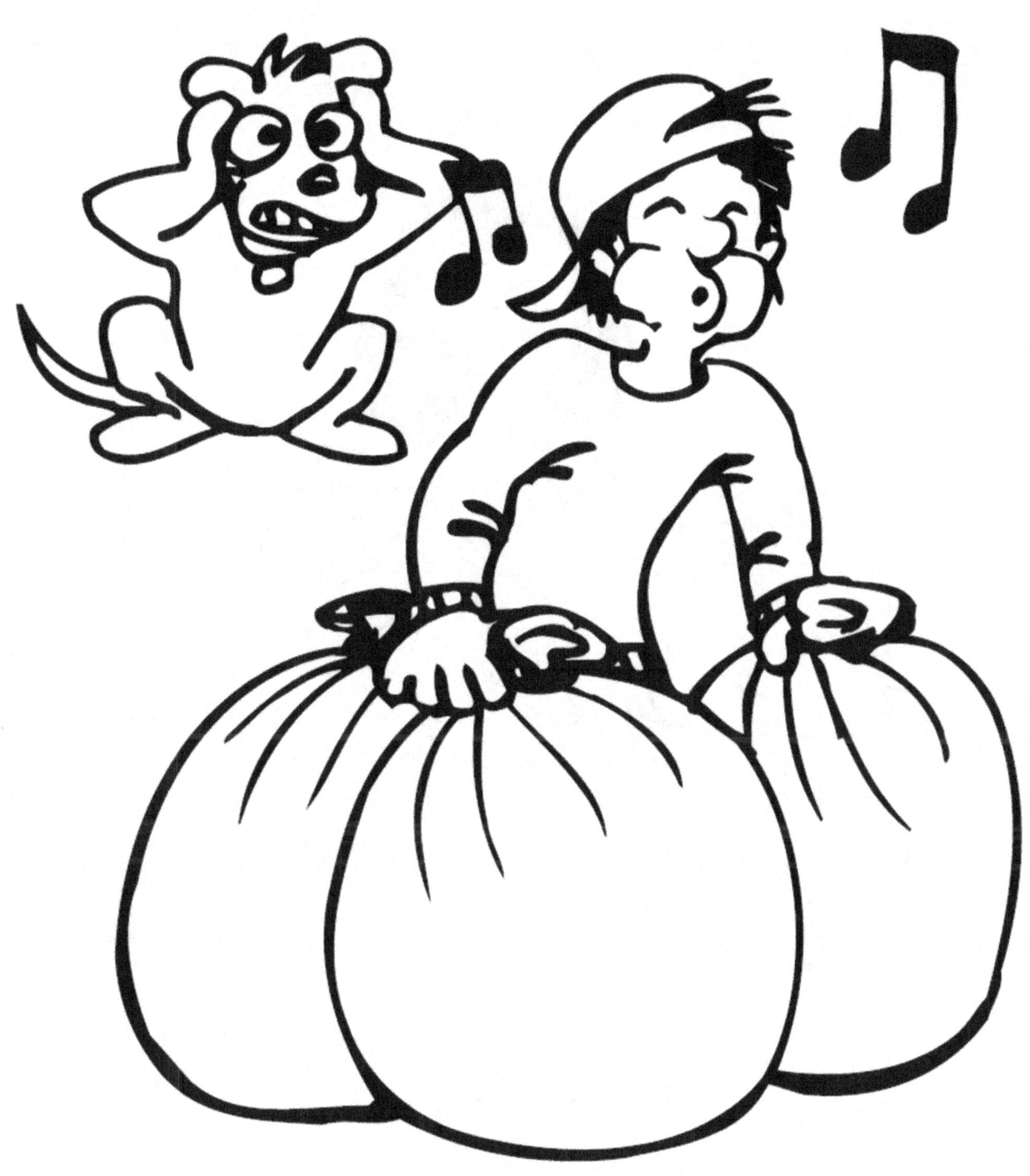

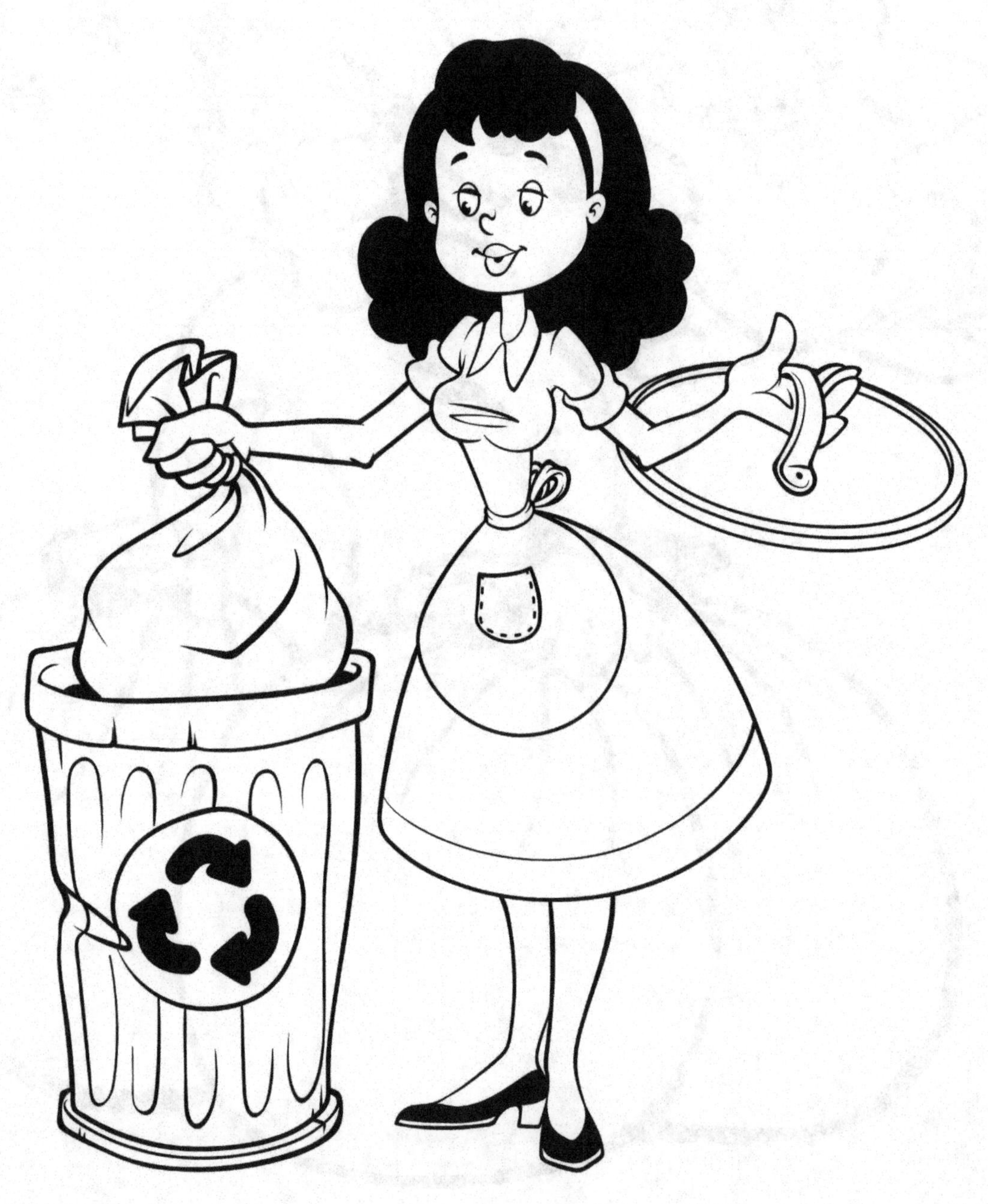

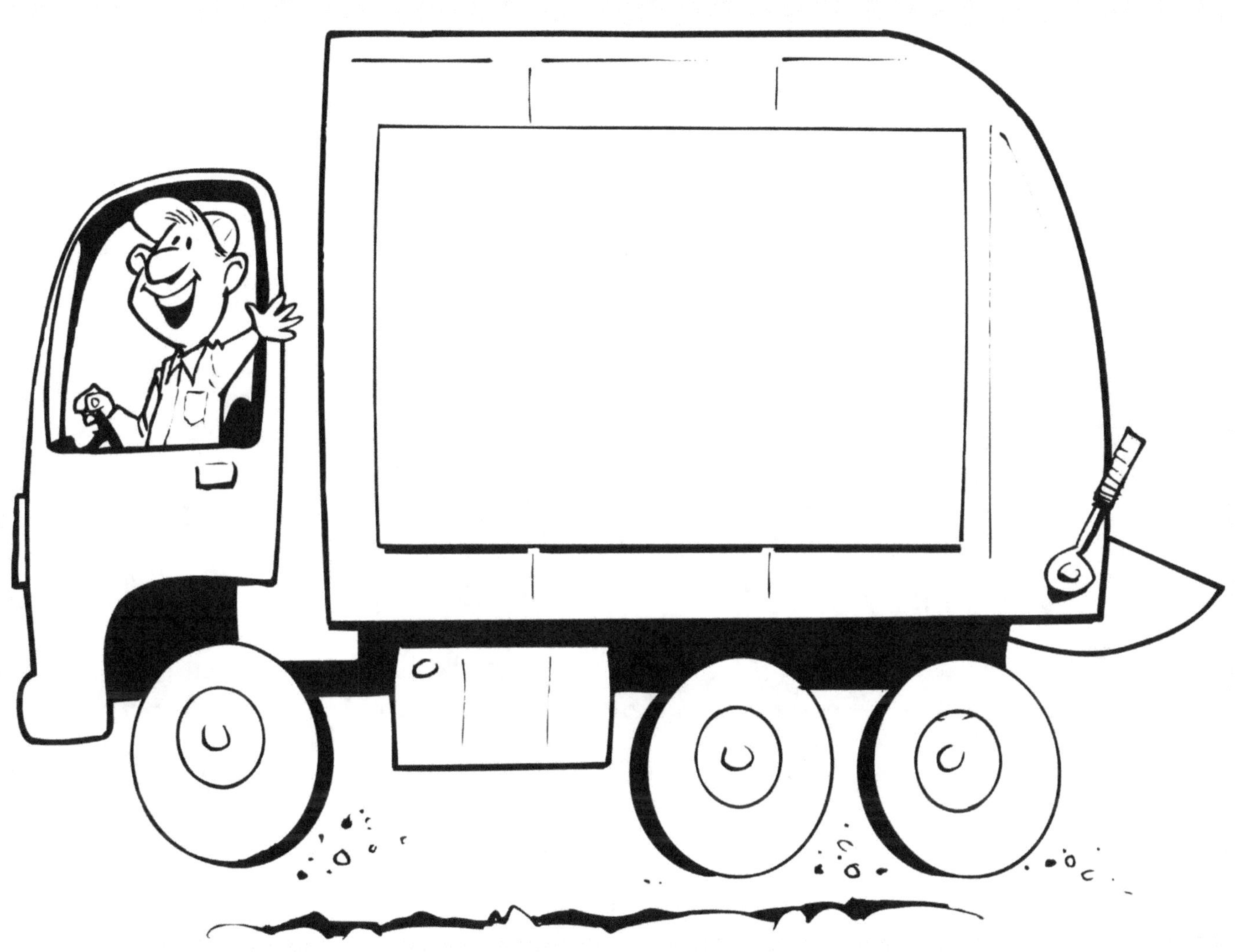

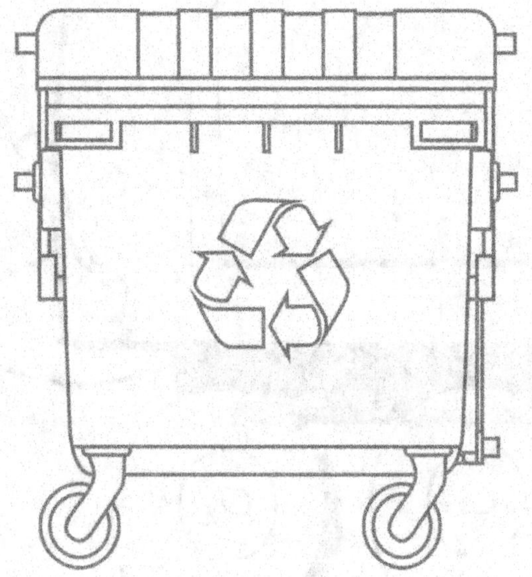 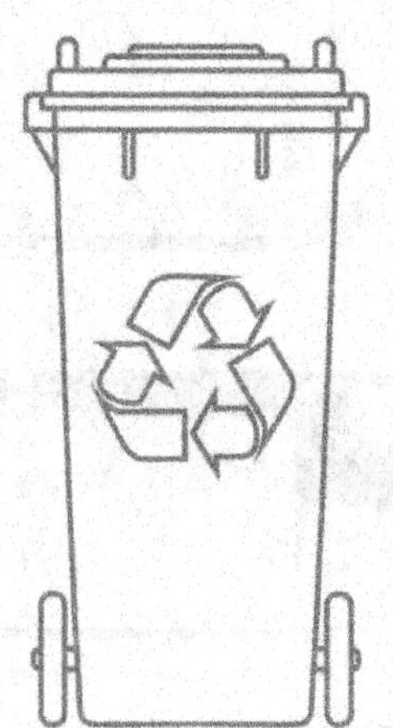 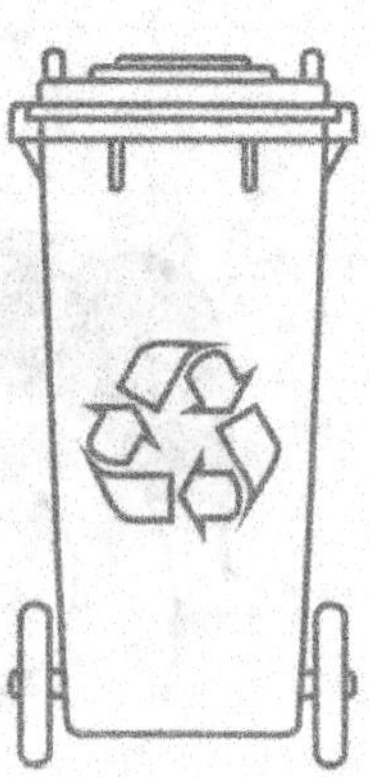

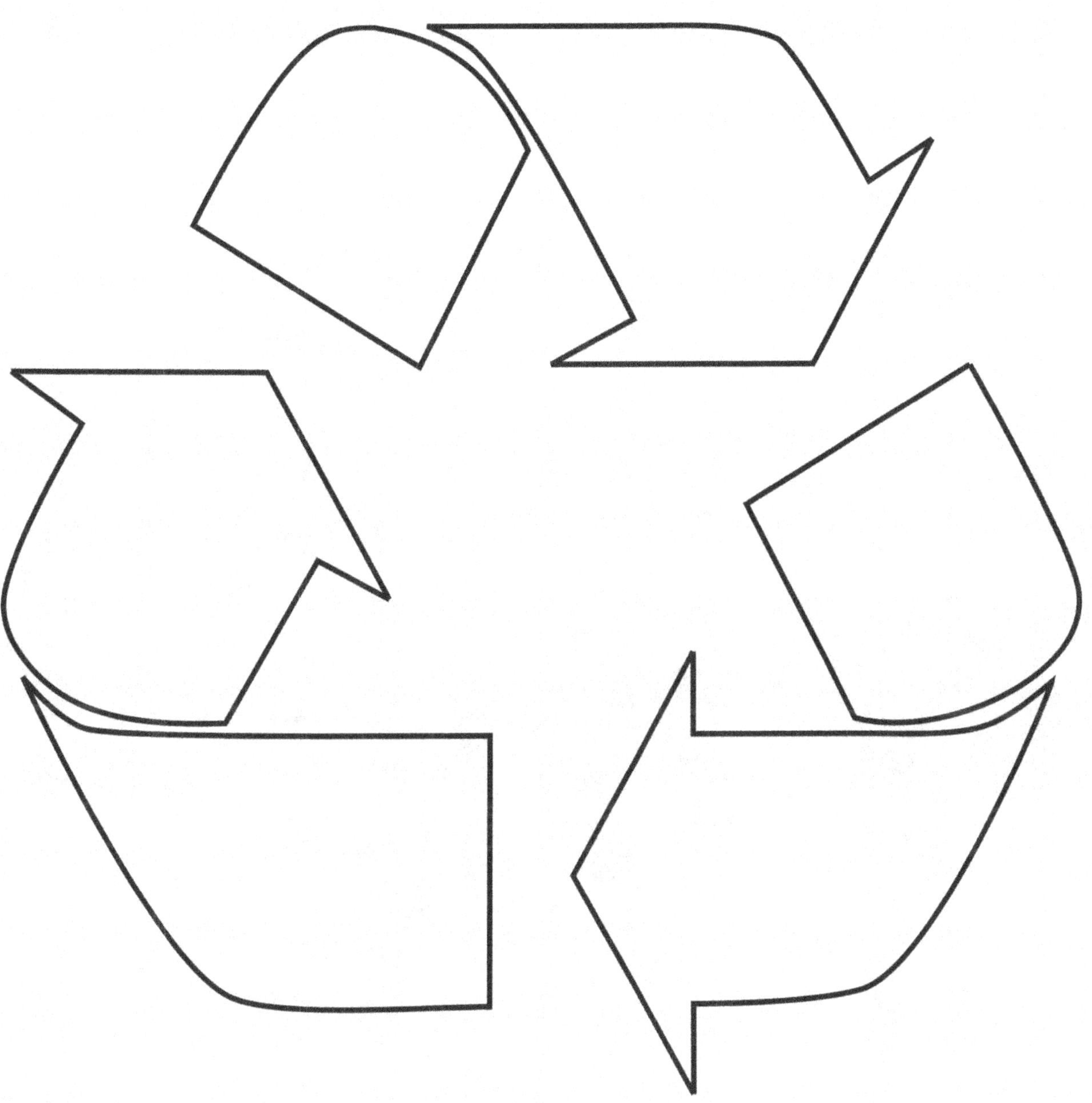

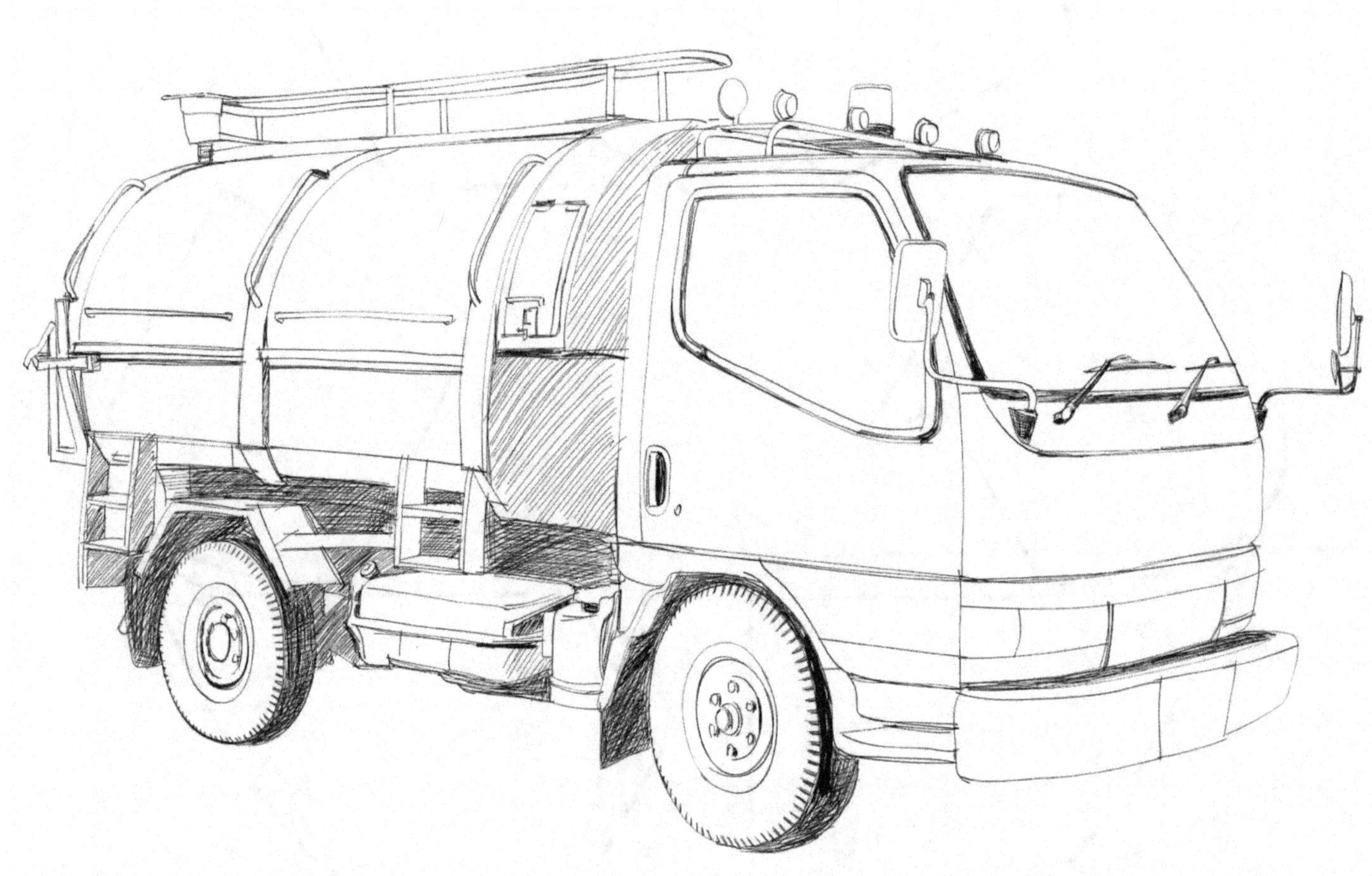

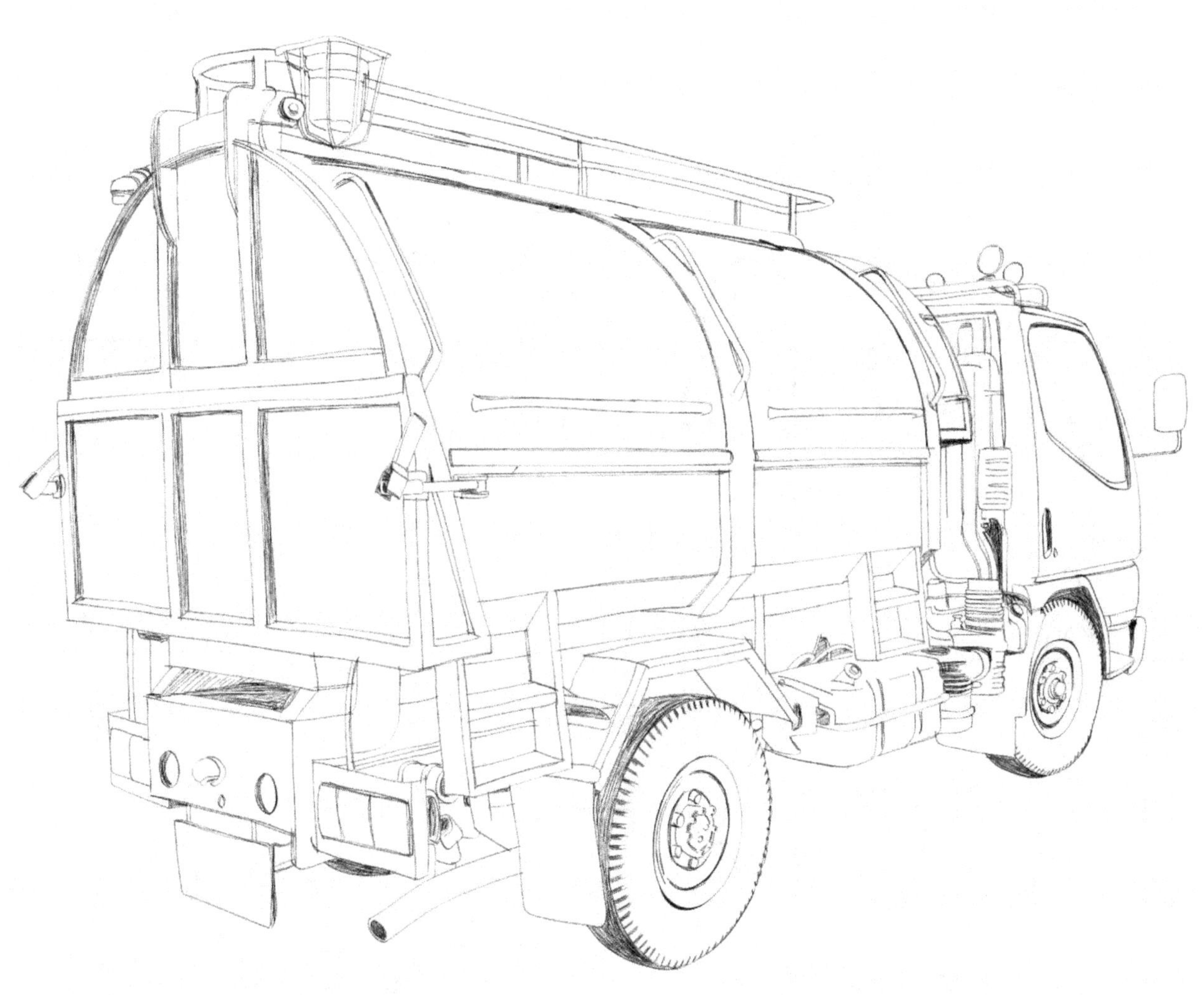

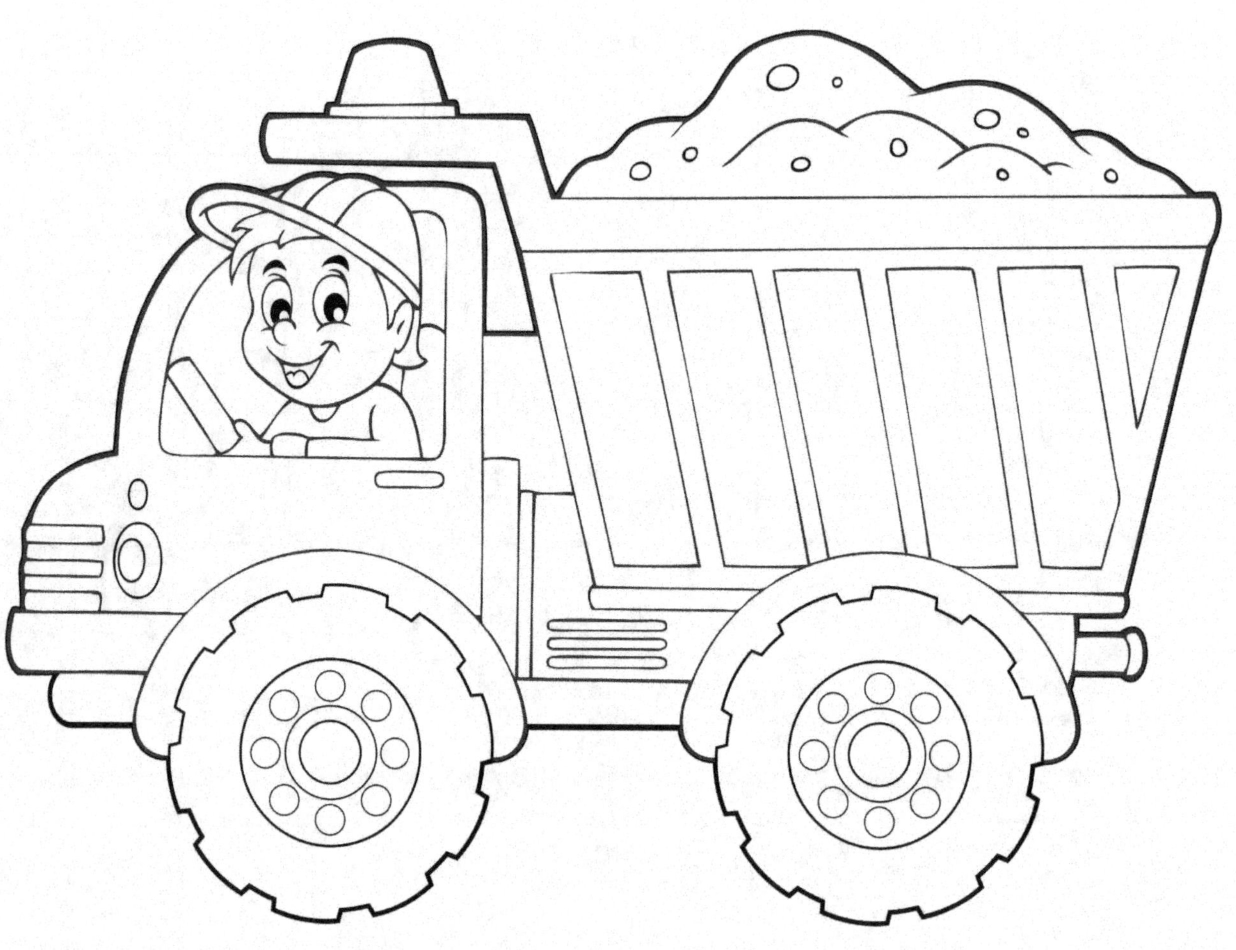

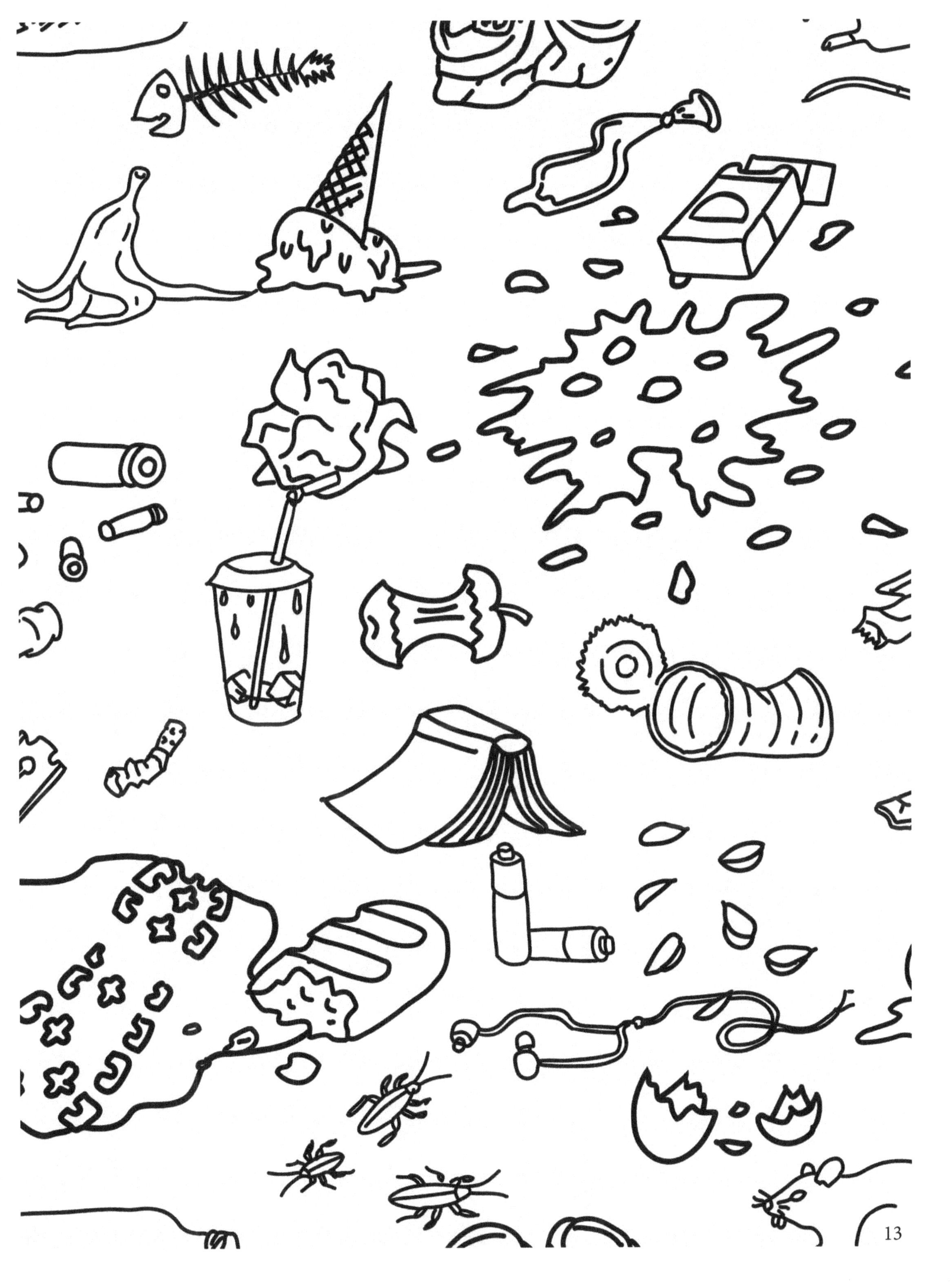

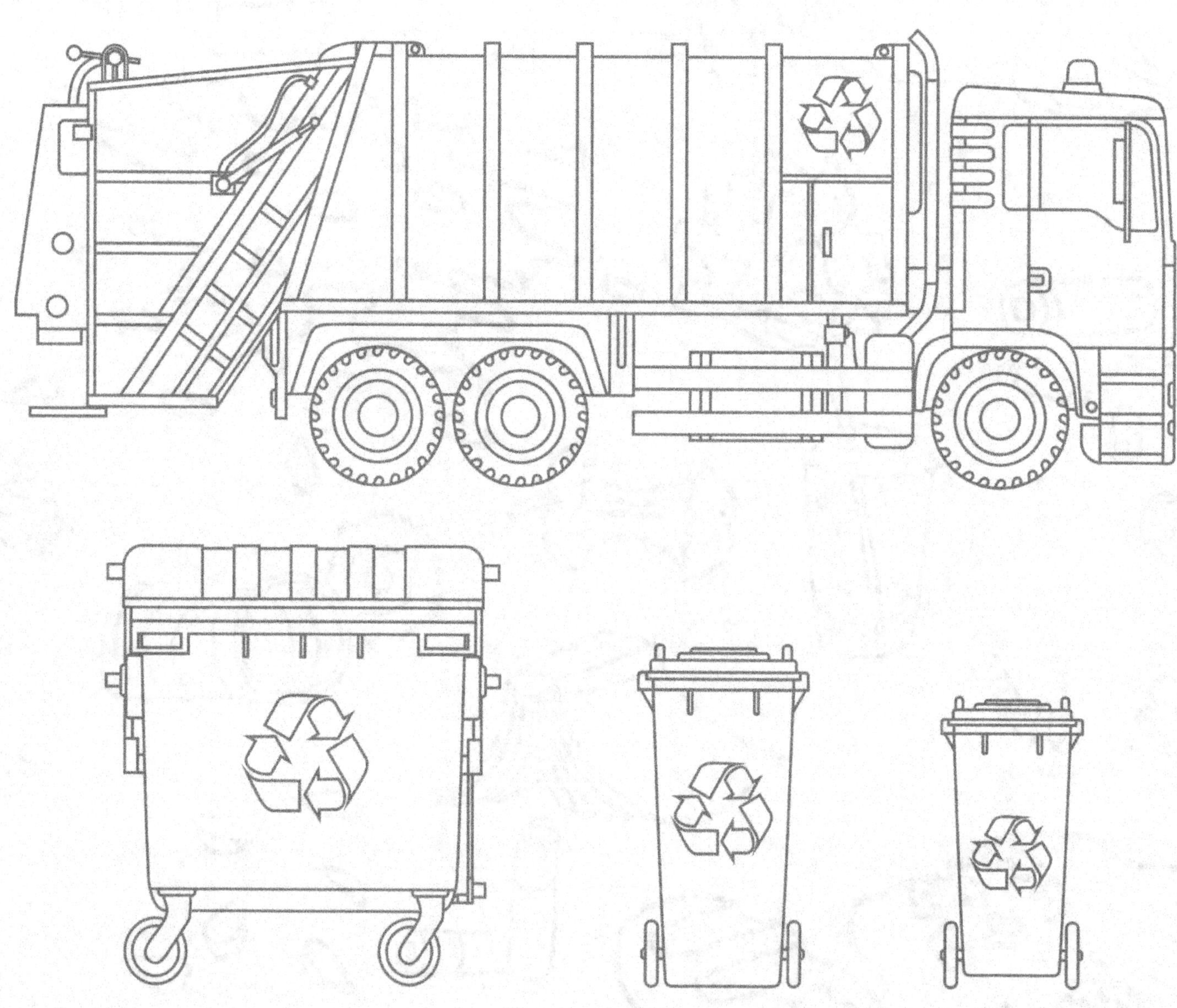

PLASTIK
WASTE
GLASS
PAPER

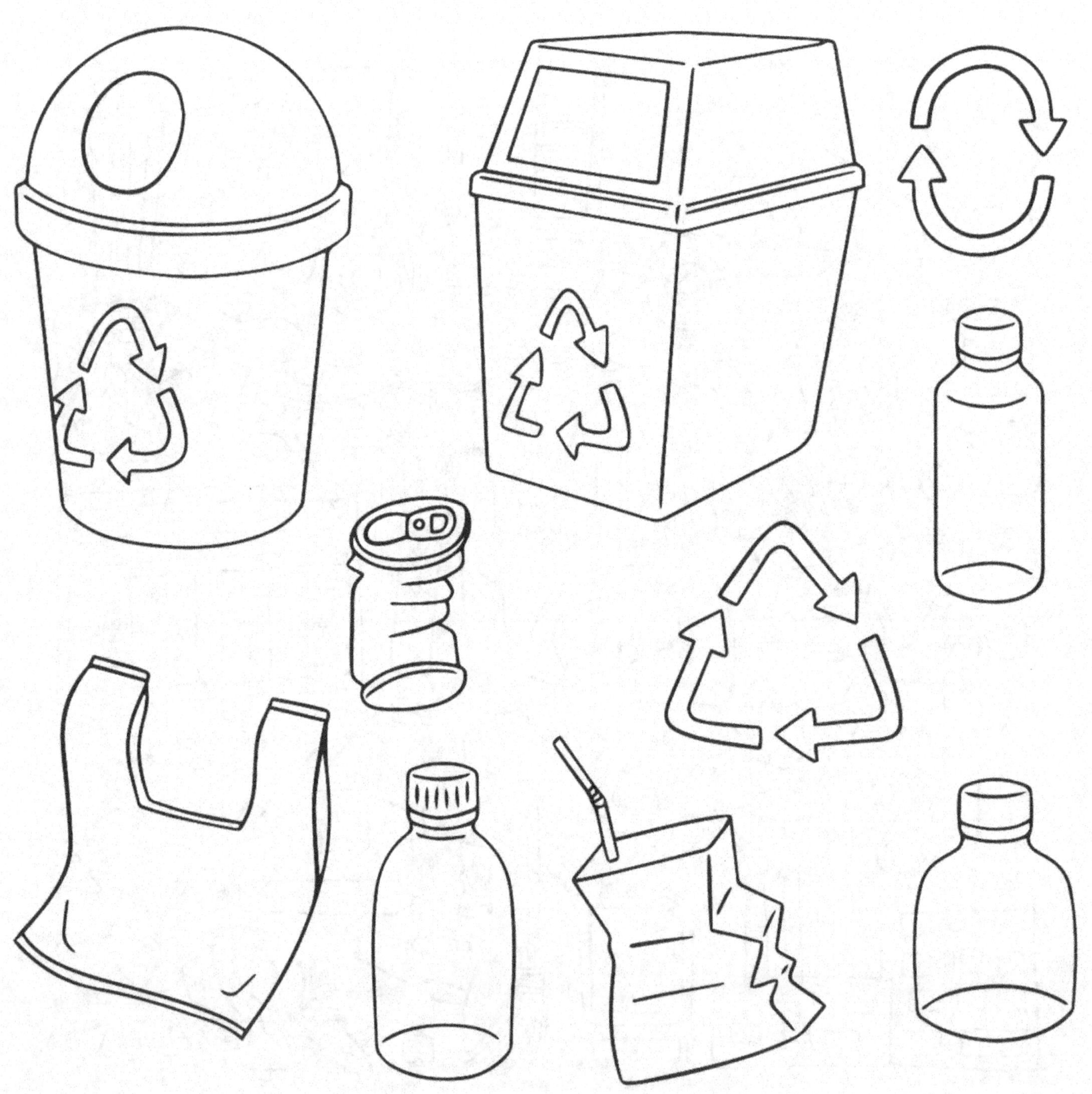

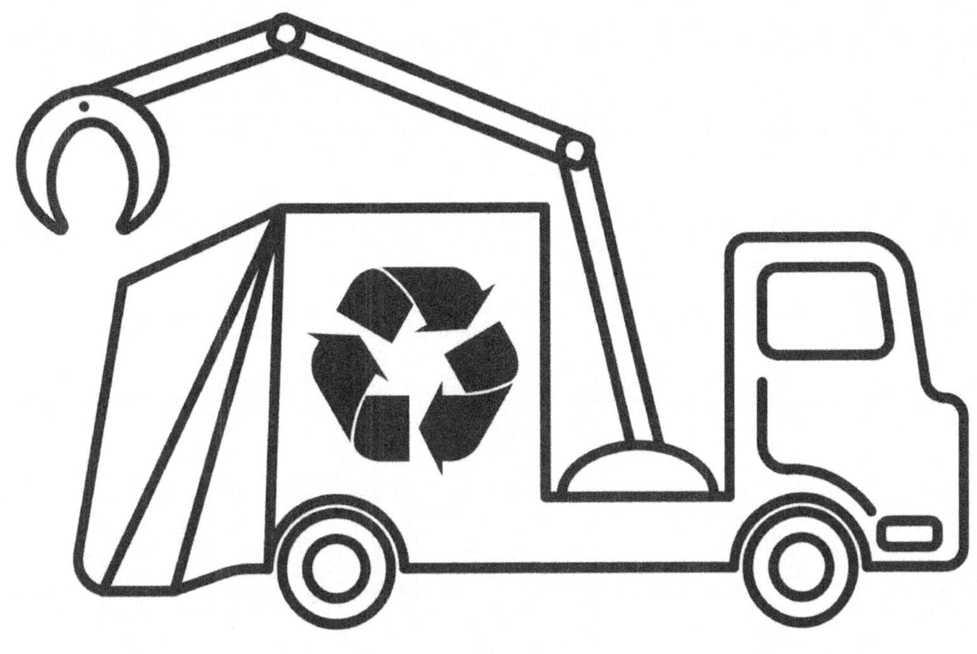

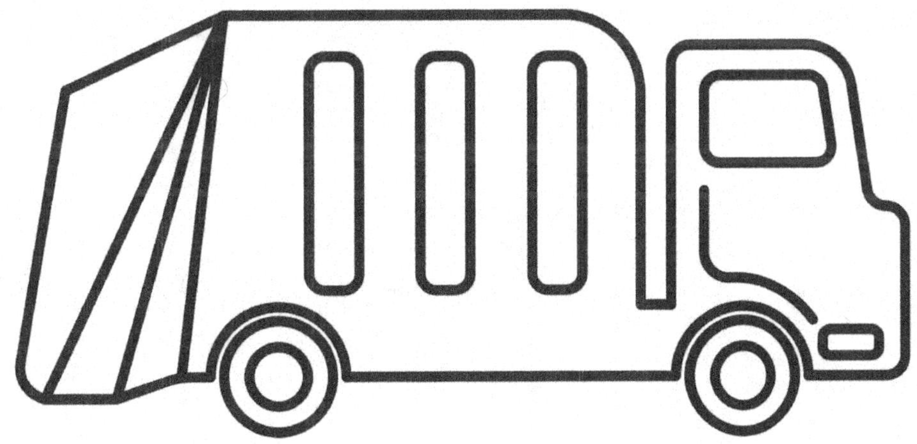

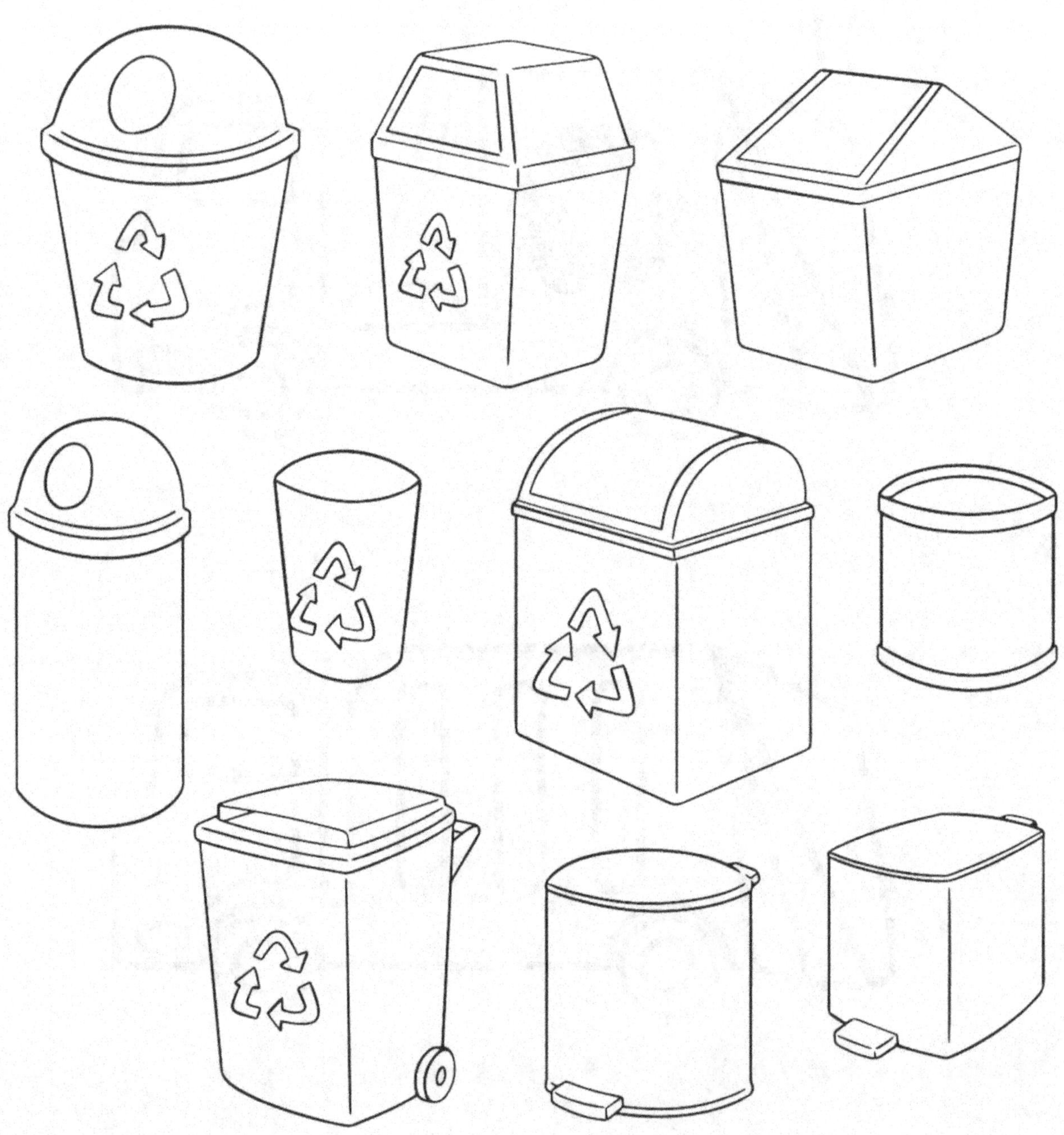

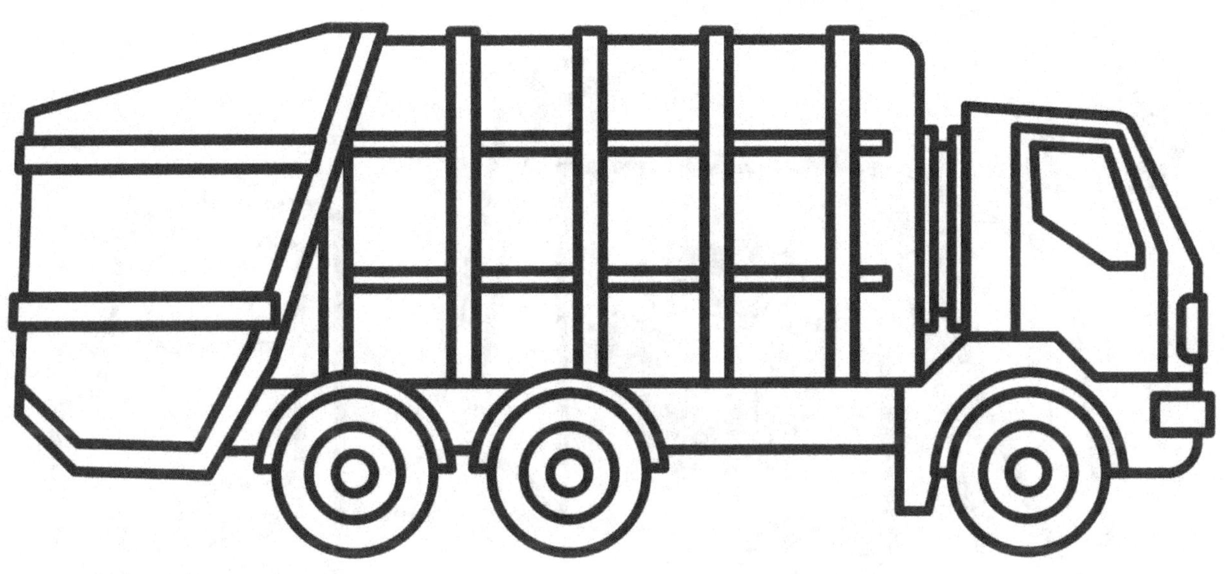

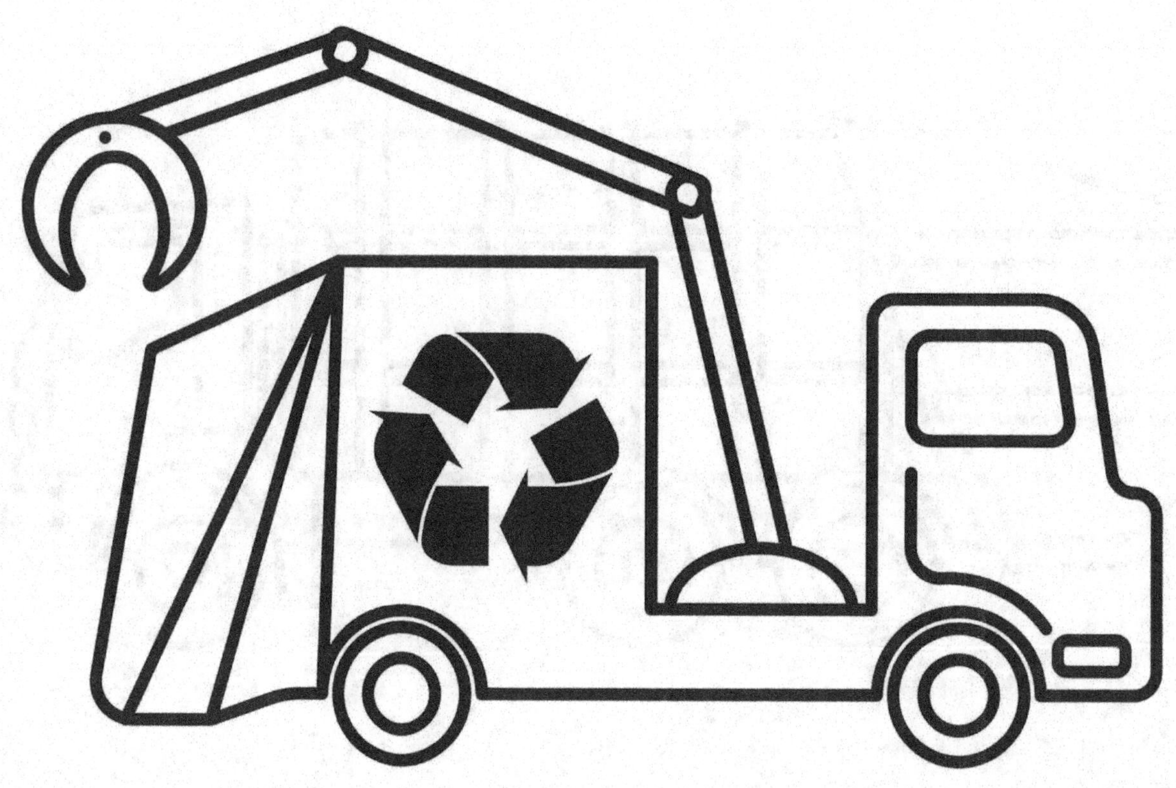

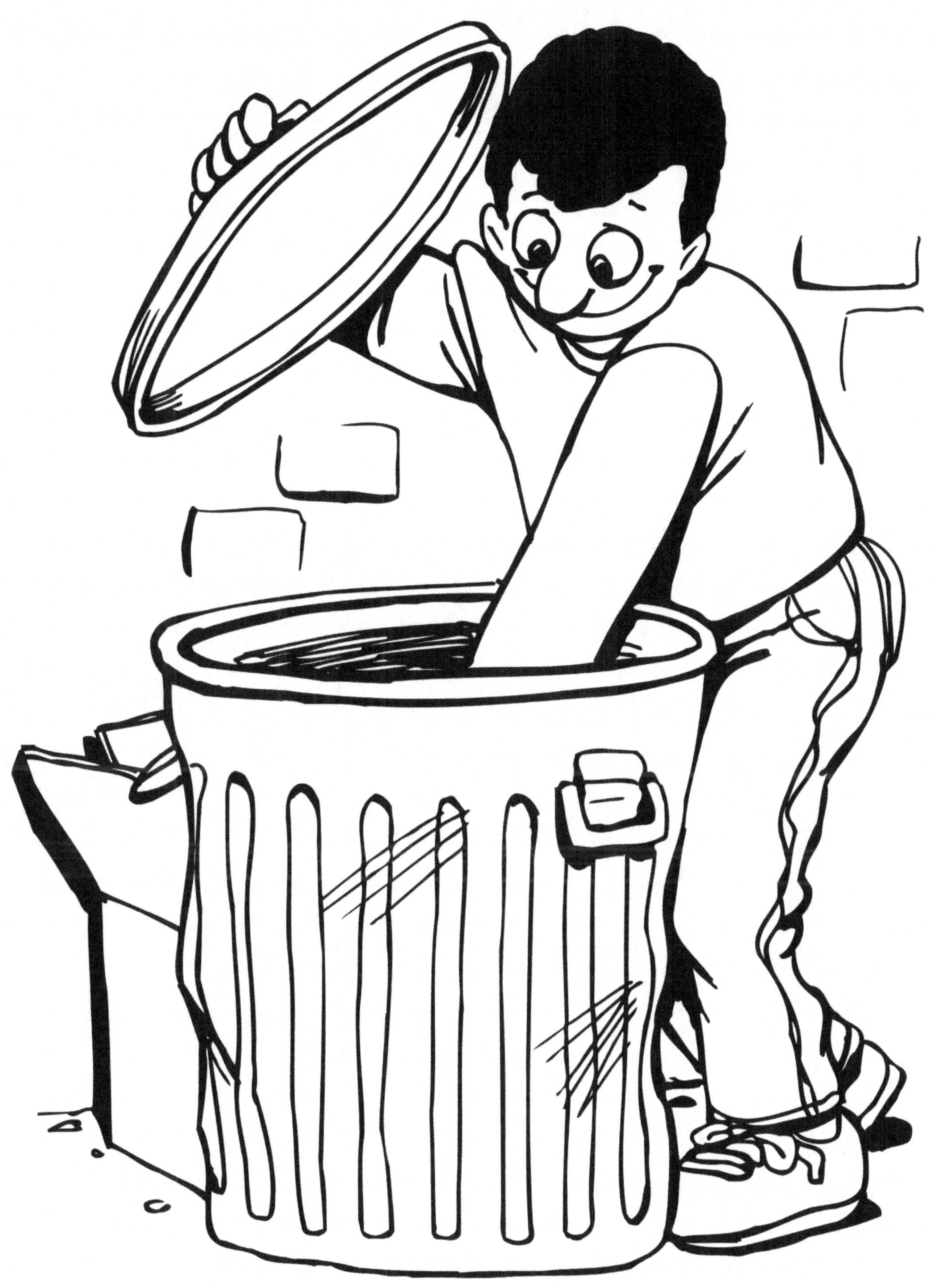

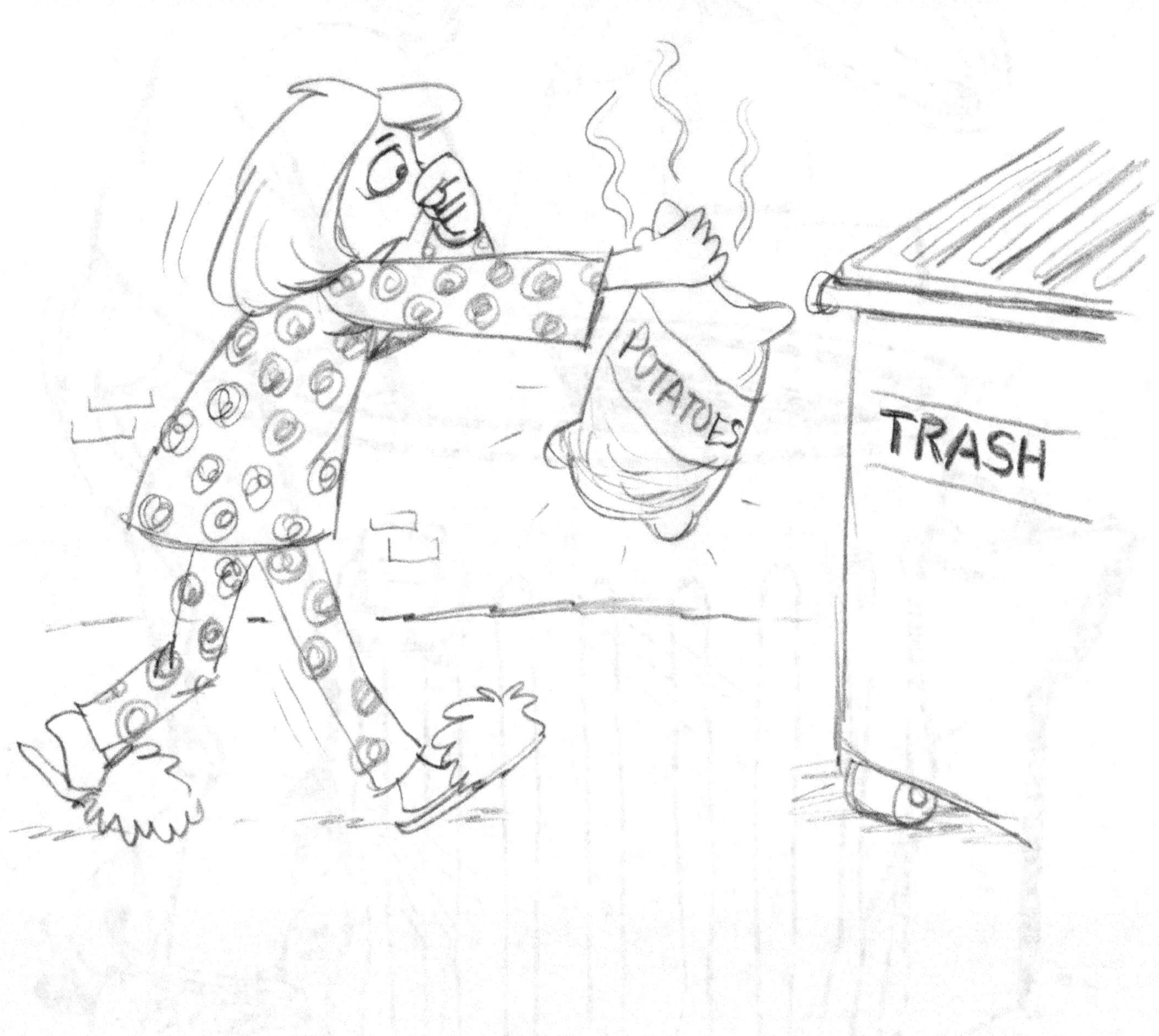
POTATOES
TRASH